MW00951777

EXPLORE ANCIENT WORLDS

ANCIENT ATHENS

AMIE JANE LEAVITT

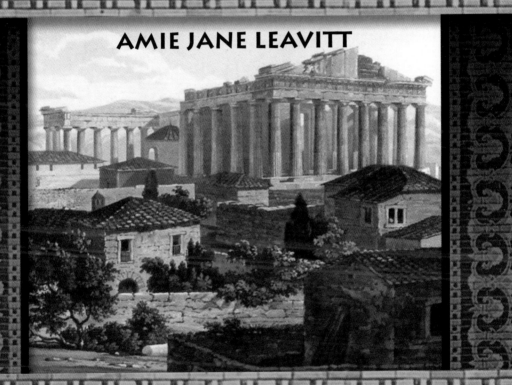

Mitchell Lane
PUBLISHERS

P.O. Box 196
Hockessin, Delaware 19707
Visit us on the web: www.mitchelllane.com
Comments? email us: mitchelllane@mitchelllane.com

EXPLORE ANCIENT WORLDS

Ancient Assyria • Ancient Athens
The Aztecs • Ancient Babylon
The Byzantine Empire • The Celts of the British Isles
Ancient China • Ancient Egypt
Ancient India/Maurya Empire • Ancient Sparta

ABOUT THE AUTHOR: Amie Jane Leavitt is an
accomplished author and photographer.
She has written more than 40 books for kids.
Leavitt particularly enjoyed writing this book
on ancient Athens since she has a great-uncle
who immigrated from Greece in the early
1900s. To check out a listing of her current
projects and other published works, check out
her web site at www.amiejaneleavitt.com.

PUBLISHER'S NOTE: The facts on which the story
in this book is based have been thoroughly
researched. Documentation of such research
can be found on page 45. While every
possible effort has been made to ensure
accuracy, the publisher will not assume liability
for damages caused by inaccuracies in the
data, and makes no warranty on the accuracy
of the information contained herein.

Printing 1 2 3 4 5 6 7 8 9

**Library of Congress
Cataloging-in-Publication Data**
Leavitt, Amie Jane.
  Ancient Athens / by Amie Jane Leavitt.
    p. cm. — (Explore ancient worlds)
  Includes bibliographical references and index.
  ISBN 978-1-61228-275-6 (library bound)
  1. Greece—Civilization—To 146 B.C.—Juvenile
literature. 2. Athens (Greece)—Social life
and customs—Juvenile literature. 3. Athens
(Greece)—Civilization—Juvenile literature. I.
Title.
  DF77.L366 2012
  938'.5--dc23
                                            2012008635

eBook ISBN: 9781612283500

PLB

CONTENTS

Acropolis of Athens by Leo von Klenze

CHAPTER
1

A Grand Celebration

The first rays of early morning light glisten off the white walls of your mud-brick home. You squint into the golden sunlight looking past the roof's smooth red tiles into the cerulean sky. It's a beautiful summer day in Athens and the weather is just perfect to celebrate the goddess Athena's birthday at the Grand Panathenaia Festival. It's your favorite festival, and since it's only celebrated in this majestic fashion every four years, you can hardly wait for the revelry to begin.

You hurry to help your mother finish the morning chores around the house. Then you help pack the family's lunch of olives, pomegranates, goat cheese, and figs to take with you to the festival. Your father is already at the agora, or marketplace, saving your family a spot along the parade route.

You cling tightly to your younger brother's hand as you follow your mother through the crowded city streets. You make your way past men pushing carts of food. You brush past soldiers, farmers, businessmen, foreigners, and dignified Athenian citizens in their grandest attire. Just like you, they're all trying to make their way to the parade route before the grand processional begins.

After nearly losing your mother twice in the sea of excited Athenians, you finally see your father waving from a spot across the street near a vendor selling amphoras, or ceramic vases, filled with olive oil. You rush to his side just in time. The processional has begun.

The cavalrymen donned in bright cloaks start the parade by clomping along the main thoroughfare on their finest horses. They're followed by glistening chariots carrying priests and noblemen. Chiseled athletes, who will compete later in the festival's games, stride along the street in their white flowing chitons with their heads adorned in crowns of laurel leaves. The city's political leaders march past and fan the crowd with olive branches. They are followed by women who carry baskets and ceramic bowls which will be used later in the sacrifice for Athena.[1]

Once the dignitaries have all marched past, the most important part of the processional begins: the presentation of Athena's new peplos, or robe. Hooked to large wooden rollers, wheels, and a tall mast, the silky golden embroidered fabric waves through the air like the sail on a ship. It cascades high above the city streets towards the Acropolis. It must have taken hundreds of hours to make such an elaborate garment. But nothing is too good for the goddess Athena. After all, she has watched over and protected your beloved city for centuries and deserves to have only the best.

When the golden fabric has sailed past, your family joins the rest of the Athenians in following the processional up the steep slope to the top of the Acropolis. This is where

An example of a peplos

6

The Parthenon has a rectangular floor plan with Doric style columns. A frieze, or horizontal band of sculpted figures, was included near the roof line. Some scholars think this frieze depicts the Grand Panathenaic processional.

Athena's statue resides, inside the temple called the Parthenon. There are too many people around you for you to see into the temple, so your father explains what is happening. The priests are carefully folding the peplos and laying it at Athena's feet.[2] Then they present her with a special sacrifice of 100 animals. The priests stand at the entrance to the temple by the great white pillars. You hear the people cheer as the priests proudly proclaim that Athena has graciously accepted the people's gift and sacrifice. Now, the celebration can begin.

You and your family find a spot to rest in the shade of an old olive tree. After a while, the slaves distribute the sacrificial meat to the waiting crowd on large bronze platters. Once your family has received its portion, you dine on the delicacy along with the fruit and cheese that your mother packed from home. Meat is a rarity in Athens, so you savor each juicy bite.

Later in the afternoon, your family returns back down to the area near the agora to watch the sideshows. You see burly men swallowing all sorts of unusual things like balls of fire and long sharp swords. You see athletes demonstrating gymnastic and acrobatic feats. At each show, you clap and cheer loudly at the death-defying displays. You watch eagerly at each interesting event until the sun makes its descent into the western horizon.

The Athens Agora

Masks were an essential part of Greek theatrical productions. They allowed actors to transform into a variety of characters during the show.

The day may be over, but the festival isn't. It continues on for eleven more days. During that time, you get to watch all sorts of athletic events like wrestling, boxing, chariot racing, javelin throwing, boat racing, and foot racing. You get to listen to musical competitions and watch theatrical productions where actors wear comical masks. And every evening you get to dine on some of the most delicious food you have ever tasted. Every day of the festival, you take special notice to look into the faces of your fellow Athenians at each of the events. You can tell by the delight on their smiling faces that they too are just as proud of their city as you are.

If you had lived in Athens during ancient times, you would have most likely attended the Grand Panathenaia Festival many times during your lifetime. Religion was very important to the ancient Athenians. They worshipped many gods and goddesses and wrote stories and legends about

In Greek mythology, gods and goddesses were given human qualities just like this statue of the goddess Athena.

them. For the people of Athens, Athena was one of the most important deities. They believed that she protected and watched over their city and helped them be both happy and prosperous.[3]

So, you may be wondering. Where exactly is Athens? What was its weather like? What kind of government did it have? And what would it have been like to live here thousands of years ago?

A Magnificent Statue

The enormous statue of Athena in the center of the Parthenon in ancient times was approximately 40 feet tall—about the size of a modern four-story building. She was so tall that during Panathenaia there was no way the people could drape her in the special peplos (robe). They just had to fold it up and place it at her feet instead.[4]

The Athena replica statue

Work on the statue began in 447 BCE under the direction of the noted Athenian sculptor Phidias. The statue was made out of ivory and gold. According to estimates, the gold alone weighed more than a ton. The face, arms, and feet of the statue were made out of ivory. The rest, which would have been her clothing, was made out of gold leaf. Athena had a snake slithering up on the inside of her shield, a small statue of the goddess Victory resting in the palm of her right hand, and a helmet of horses crowning her head.

The original statue no longer exists but replicas are found in various places around the world. The two copies that look the most like the original are found in museums in Rome and Athens. Another one stands in Nashville, Tennessee. The work of American sculptor Alan LeQuire, the statue took eight years to complete and was put on display in 1990.

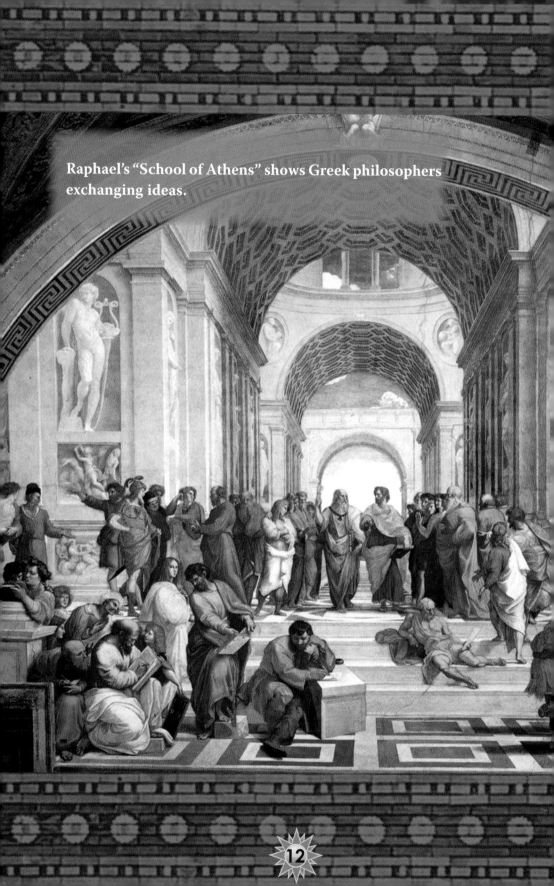

Raphael's "School of Athens" shows Greek philosophers exchanging ideas.

CHAPTER 2

A City Protected by Athena

Today Athens is the largest city in Greece and the country's capital. In ancient times, Greece wasn't a unified country, so it didn't have a capital. It was actually made up of many city-states. A city-state was an area that was independent and more like a very small country. In ancient Greece, there were approximately 1,500 different city-states spread out along the Mediterranean and Black Sea. The famous Greek philosopher Plato once said that these cities were "like frogs around a pond."[1] While the city-states all shared the same language, they each had their own government, culture, and customs and were oftentimes at war with each other.

Athens was one of the most important of all the city-states. While its rival, the city-state of Sparta, was best known for its militaristic lifestyle, Athens was particularly known for its arts and culture. It was also known for its form of government. Around 510 BCE, the people of Athens decided to form a government where the people made the laws instead of a king or a small group of ruling noblemen. This revolutionary idea made Athens the birthplace of democracy, or government by the people. Democracy comes from the Greek word demokratia, which means "people power."[2]

Greece is located in southern Europe at the southern tip of the Balkan Peninsula. A peninsula is an area of land that is surrounded on three sides by water. The Balkan Peninsula is surrounded by the waters of the Adriatic Sea, the Mediterranean Sea, the Sea of Crete, the Aegean Sea, and the Black

Sea. Modern-day Greece is made up of land on the peninsula (called the mainland) plus hundreds of nearby islands. The country has about 8,500 miles of coastline.[3] Because of this, sea travel for transportation and trade has always been very important to the Greeks. Athens was connected to the sea by the nearby port city of Piraeus, which was about 7.5 miles away.

Greece is one of the most mountainous countries in all of Europe. In fact, it's estimated that 80 percent of Greece is made up of mountains. Mount Olympus is the highest point in the country. It stands at 9,576 feet above sea level. In ancient times, it was on Mount Olympus that the Greeks believed their gods lived. You may recognize the name Olympus—that's where the Olympic Games got its name.[4]

The city of Athens is located on mainland Greece in the southeastern part of the country. It's situated on a plain surrounded by hills and mountains. In the center of the city is a rocky hill called the Acropolis. In

Greek, "acro" means "high" and "polis" means "city." This is where the original city was built since it was a spot high enough to provide protection from outside invaders. Eventually, the city spread out into the area below the Acropolis. All of this, plus the farmland that surrounded the city, became the city-state of Athens. The Acropolis was home to many important buildings, including the temple called the Parthenon. This religious edifice is where the ancient Athenians came to worship their gods.

Athens has what is called a "Mediterranean climate." This is similar to the climate in parts of the state of California. The summers, which last from April to October, are hot and dry. The winters, which last from November until March, are mild and wet.

If you lived in ancient Greece, chances were good that you would have probably been a farmer. That's because about 80 percent of ancient Athenians were farmers. At first, the farmers in this region mainly grew wheat. But soon the soil became overworked and this grain crop became difficult to grow. So they decided to plant olive trees, which was actually a really great idea. In ancient times, olives were eaten as food. Olive oil was used for cooking and for lighting candles. It was also used as a lotion on athletes to make them look shiny and more muscular. If you had olives or olive oil to sell, you could make a great deal of money. Along with olives, the region also grew barley, grapes, fruit, and vegetables.[5]

Ancient Athenians were quite healthy eaters. They usually only ate red meats on special occasions, and consumed fish, grains, fruits, and vegetables on a daily basis. Some of the most important foods in their diet were honey, eggs, figs, dates, olives, olive oil, fish, pomegranates, cereals, cabbage, chickpeas, peas, beans, onions, and lentils.

Residents of ancient Athens typically ate only small meals throughout the day, with a large meal in the evening. When they rose from bed in the morning, they'd have either some wheat or barley bread dipped in olive oil or wine. Then, around noon, they'd have some leftovers from the night before or more bread accompanied by cheese, dried fish, olives, figs, or other fruit. At night, when all of the business of the day was finished, they would return home and eat a larger meal of vegetables, fish, fruit, more bread, and honey cakes called sweetmeats.

Anselm Feuerbach (1829–1880) painted this scene from Plato's Symposium in 1869.

The men would generally eat in one area of the house and the women would eat in another. Oftentimes, the men would invite their friends over for a dinner party called a symposium. They would eat together, listen to flute or harp music, sing songs, play games, and then talk politics, philosophy, or religion. The women and children would eat together in their part of the house. After everyone else was fed, the slaves would eat their meager portions in their part of the house.

The ancient Athenians didn't have utensils like forks and spoons. They ate with their hands and often used slices of bread to scoop up mouthfuls of food. This style of eating is still practiced in parts of the world today in such places as Morocco, Ethiopia, and Nepal.

Who was Athena?

In ancient Greek mythology, Athena is the goddess of the useful arts like farming, spinning, and weaving. She is also the goddess of wisdom and warfare.

Even though Athena was the goddess of warfare, she was actually known to be slow to anger. This fit in perfectly with the temperament of the ancient Athenians. That's because unlike their Spartan neighbors, they preferred to fight out their battles with words and wisdom rather than with the sword. When Athens had to go to war, though, it was believed that Athena protected their cities, states, and soldiers.

Athena and Zeus

According to the ancient myth, Athena was the daughter of Zeus and Metis. She was born out of the head of her father. When she was born, she was wearing the robe and helmet that her mother had made for her. Zeus was very happy that Athena was a girl. He feared that a son would try to take over his kingdom. Athena remained one of his favorite children throughout his life. When she was older, he gave her a special shield called the aegis. On the front of the shield was the face of Medusa—the monster that had snakes for hair. When anyone looked at Medusa's face, they died. This helped protect Athena from her enemies.[6]

Family homes surround the Acropolis as the Parthenon is constructed in this illustration.

So what would it have been like to live in ancient Athens? To a large extent, that depended upon who you were. Wealthy citizens, foreigners, children, women, and slaves all lived very different lives.

Historians believe that people have been living in the site of Athens for more than 6,000 years. During its peak, which was roughly between 500 and 400 BCE, there were probably between 250,000 and 300,000 people living in Athens. This made Athens the largest city-state in all of Greece.[1]

Citizens were the most important group of people in ancient Athens. Yet, not everyone in Athens actually qualified as a citizen. First, your parents had to be born in Athens. Second, you had to be born in Athens. Third, you had to have served in the military if you wanted to vote in elections. Fourth, you had to be at least 20 years of age. All in all, only about one-third of the population of Athens was citizens or members of a citizen's family.

Wealthy men in Athens had it the best, especially if they were citizens. They could vote in elections and decide the laws of the city. They could discuss politics in the marketplace. They could be educated, own property, have jobs outside the home, serve on juries and in the Assembly, and run for public office.

If you were a man with little money in Athens, you wouldn't have all of these opportunities, even if you were a citizen. For one, education required money. And, if you didn't have money, it would be difficult to buy property.

Women in ancient Athens had very few rights. They were expected to stay inside the home and cook, clean, weave, and take care of the children. Women could not vote. They could not own property. They could not be formally educated. They could occasionally go to special festivals, like the Grand Panathenaia, but most other times they needed to stay home. There was very little outside the home that they were even allowed to do on their own without an escort. They didn't even get to choose who they married. At the age of fourteen or fifteen, their fathers would choose a suitable husband for them.[2]

Women were in charge of household duties like raising children and embroidering fabric. The cleaning would have likely been the job of the slaves.

Life was considerably less strict for women in neighboring Sparta. Women in this ancient Greek city-state could own property. They were taught how to read and write. And they could even participate in athletic competitions.[3]

Slaves in Athens, both male and female, had very few, if any rights. Their time, their lives, and all the effort they put into their work belonged to someone else. Sometimes people were born slaves. At other times, they became slaves when their country was defeated in war. And still other times, people became slaves when they could not pay the debts that they owed.[4] According to estimates, as much as 40 percent of the population of Athens may have been slaves.

In ancient Athens, only wealthy boys were formally educated. In school, each subject was taught by a different teacher who specialized in that topic. Early on, students learned how to read and write. They practiced writing their letters and words on special wooden tablets that were coated with a thin layer of wax. They wrote on the wax with a pointed pen-like object called a stylus. Music was also an important subject in ancient Athens. Students learned how to play an instrument called a lyre. This pear-shaped stringed instrument was very similar in shape and appearance to a small harp. In addition to the lyre, students learned how to play the flute.

Physical education was important in ancient Athens. Students learned how to ride horses and box. They were trained in wrestling and gymnastics. Students were also schooled in art, drama, public speaking, politics, and mathematics. They generally stayed in a formal school until the age of 18 or 20.[5]

Children in ancient Athens did have fun when they weren't helping with chores around the house or going to school. They played with toys such as dolls, yo-yos, hoops, rattles, balls, and wooden horses.[6] They played games similar to modern-day marbles and blind man's bluff. They also had pets like dogs, geese, and chickens.[7]

For the most part, regardless of their status, people wore the same basic type of clothing: loose-fitting robes made of lightweight materials. That's because of the climate. People usually wear clothes that suit the type of weather they have. In Athens, the climate was hot and dry most of the year. Men's robes were called chitons and women's were called peploi (singular peplos). These were both made out of large rectangular pieces of either linen or wool fabric and were attached at the shoulders with pins. Wealthy women would often wear jewelry with their peploi, such as gold necklaces and headbands in their hair.[8]

Athenians often went barefoot, especially inside their houses. They also wore leather sandals that laced up past the ankles or lightweight leather boots.

In "Saint Paul Preaching in Athens" by Raphael, we get a glimpse of how men dressed in ancient Athens.

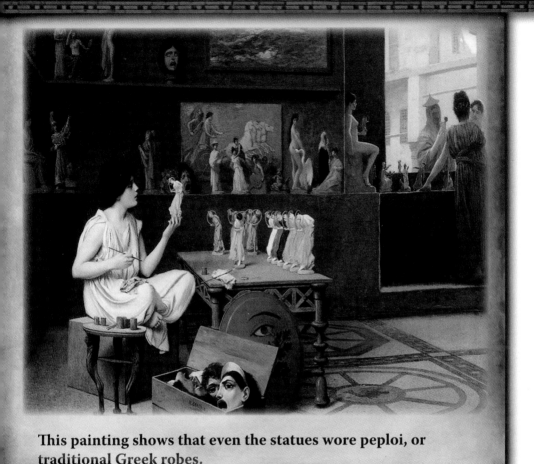

This painting shows that even the statues wore peploi, or traditional Greek robes.

People in ancient Athens lived in houses that suited the climate. Most homes were white in color and were built out of thick mud bricks. They were built in a rectangular shape around an opening in the middle called the courtyard. All of the rooms of the house opened into the courtyard and just had small slits for windows on the outside walls.

In ancient Athens, a part of the house was specifically for the men and another part of the house was for the women. The men ate on the main floor. This is also where they entertained their guests. The women's area was generally found upstairs in a back corner room. This is where they ate and sewed and took care of the children. Homes also had an indoor bath

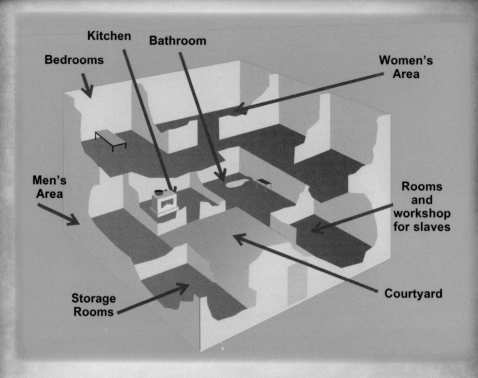

Kitchen

Bathroom

Bedrooms

Women's Area

Men's Area

Rooms and workshop for slaves

Storage Rooms

Courtyard

A typical family home in ancient Athens might have looked like this illustration.

area with a tub filled by hand with water from a well, a kitchen, storage rooms, bedrooms, and workshops for slaves.

The rooms had very few furnishings. In the bedrooms, there was usually just a small chest for clothing and a cushioned couch for a bed. These same couches were found in the men's entertaining room. The women's room usually had a few chairs, a chest for storage, and a loom for weaving.[9]

The Three Great Philosophers

Plato, Socrates, and Aristotle

Socrates (469–399 BCE) was one of the first philosophers in Athens. He discussed ideas in the agora and taught them to pupils. One of his most famous students was Plato. Many of Socrates' ideas were different from the beliefs of the time period. Because of this, a number of people disliked his ideas. When he was in his late 60s, he was placed on trial. A jury of 500 Athenian citizens found him guilty, saying that he had corrupted the city's youth with his ideas and had not properly acknowledged the gods and goddesses. He was forced to drink poison as his death sentence.[10]

Plato (429–347 BCE) was both a mathematician and a scientist. Many people believe that modern western philosophy and science began with the work of Plato. He wrote many important books. His most famous was *The Republic,* which discussed laws and justice. Plato also started a school called the Academy of Athens in 387 BCE. This was the very first college in the western world. Plato's most famous student, Aristotle, studied at this college for twenty years.

After leaving the Academy of Athens, Aristotle (384–322 BCE) started another school called the Lyceum. He was also the private tutor of Alexander the Great. Some people think Aristotle was one of the most important people who ever lived. He had advanced knowledge on all types of topics including natural science, logic, ethics, and politics.

This print titled "Hippocrates Refusing the Gifts of Artaxerxes" by Massard in 1816 was based on an oil painting by Girodet from 1792.

The work was based on a legend that Hippocrates refused bribe money to treat Persian soldiers during a pandemic.

CHAPTER 4

The Golden Age

The marketplace in ancient Athens was called the agora. It lay near the base of the Acropolis and was the heart of the city. You could buy fish, honey, fruits, cheeses, eggs, olive oil, vegetables, and fish there. You could even buy things like ivory, elephants, and silk from such faraway places as Egypt, India, and China.[1]

The agora was not only where you bought food, clothing, household items, and other goods from shopkeepers but it was also where you came to talk "shop" with your fellow Athenians. You could discuss politics, philosophy, business, current events, science, and religion. It wouldn't have seemed "lady-like" for women to engage in such discussions at the agora, however. So, most of this "shop-talk" was done by men.

If you were a curious person in the ancient world, you would have wanted to go to the agora to talk to one of the three most important philosophers of the era: Socrates, Plato, and Aristotle. Socrates was the teacher of Plato and Plato was the teacher of Aristotle.[2]

Or if you preferred, you could have gone to chat about science and medicine. Both were incredibly important in ancient Athens. "The Father of Modern Medicine" was Hippocrates, an ancient Greek who was born on the Greek island of Cos. According to some reports, he came to live in Athens around 430 BCE to try to halt a plague that killed many Athenians.

Today, doctors still take the Hippocratic Oath—a promise to practice medicine ethically—which was named after Hippocrates.[3]

From about 500 to 300 BCE, Greece was in its Golden Age. During this time, people wanted to visit Athens to learn about its history, watch its democracy in action, see its famous buildings, worship in its temples, or be educated in its schools.

The leader of Athens during the start of the Golden Age was a man named Pericles, who came to power around 460 BCE. Pericles was one of Athens' most important leaders. He believed in education, the arts, and theater. He wanted to make all of these more available to Athenians regardless of how much money they had. He also wanted to build important buildings (like the Parthenon). And he thought it was important to have a strong military to protect the city from invaders. Pericles also built the Long Walls which linked Athens to its port of Piraeus.[4]

Pericles delivers a funeral oration for the victims of war. He was considered one of Athens' most important leaders.

Another important legacy of ancient Greece is the Olympics. The Olympics began in 776 BCE in the city of Olympia. Athletes from all of the city-states, including Athens, participated in horse-racing events, foot races, the long jump, discus throw, and wrestling.

The ancient Athenians were known for their impressive architecture. Today, architects still follow their classic style. Take, for example, the Parthenon. The Lincoln Memorial in Washington, D.C., was designed to look just like it. The White

A Doric column and the Lincoln Memorial

House, Supreme Court Building, and Capitol all have elements of ancient Greek style.

What does ancient Greek architecture look like? Basically, the Greeks used tall marble columns in one of three styles: Doric, Ionic, and Corinthian. The first two were the most common. The Parthenon, for example, was built using Doric columns.

Ancient Athenians loved their theater. Their plays, which were presented outdoors, fell into two categories: tragedies and comedies. Many famous tragedies were written by Aeschylus, Sophocles, and Euripides. Aristophanes was a master comic playwright. Eleven of Aristophanes' plays have survived the centuries. One, *The Clouds,* poked fun at Socrates. Another one, *The Frogs,* was so popular that it received first place in Athens' annual dramatic competition—the Lenaia festival—in 405 BCE. This play was about a journey to Hades (the underworld) and included a royal cast of characters of Greek gods such as Dionysus, Heracles, and Pluto along with people—both famous and common—animals, and slaves.[5]

In Greek theater, the actors dressed up in costumes and wore masks to show exaggerated facial expressions to the audience. That way the audience members, even those who sat far in the back of the theater, could see the emotions of the actors. In addition, since the actors were always men, the masks showed if the character was supposed to be a man or a woman, or even an animal. The masks covered the entire head and had large openings for the mouth and eyes. They were painted in bright colors and included decorations like leaves, berries, real hair, and ribbons.

During the Golden Age, the Athenians and other ancient Greeks invented things such as an accurate water clock, water wheel, odometer, alarm clock, lighthouse, wheelbarrow, plumbing, paved streets, and the crane.

The Athenians also perfected the art form of mosaic, an artwork made out of little pieces of tile or stone. They used tiny colored pebbles to create floors, walls, and ceilings in intricate designs of people, animals, and geometric shapes. Sometimes the pebbles were only a few millimeters in length. Some of these mosaics still exist today.

The Greeks didn't just make bowls, vases, and dishes for practical uses. They also made them as a way to tell a story. Most pottery had painted

pictures showing what everyday life and special events were like in the ancient world. Much of what we know about the ancient Greeks is due to this pottery. Thousands of pieces of pottery have survived—each with a different story to tell.

A Kalydonian Boar Hunt, among other stories, is depicted in this example of Greek pottery.

Greek Sculpture

The ancient Greeks were masters of the art form of sculpture. Some of the sculptures were molded out of clay and wax and then bronze was poured over the top. Others were carved directly out of marble. Many of the original Greek sculptures have been lost or destroyed over time. Luckily, the Romans liked the Greek style so much that they copied many of their pieces.

The Greeks respected the human body and used it as inspiration for their artwork. They were one of the first civilizations to do this. They

Discobolus

studied every detail of the human body which allowed them to create sculptures that were incredibly realistic. Prior to this time, sculpture was rigid and was only an imitation of the human body. Greek art during the Classical Era, however, appeared so realistic that it was almost as if the artist had somehow magically transformed a real person into marble.[6]

Greek artists often depicted bodies in motion like a person running, throwing something, or riding a horse. One of the most famous pieces of art from this time period is called Discobolus, or discus-thrower. The original Greek statue was made out of bronze. This Roman replica was carved out of marble. Look at the detail in the ribs and muscles of this athlete and the expression on his face. He looks exactly like a real person, doesn't he?

Athens today

CHAPTER 5

Visiting Ancient Athens

Politically, the great civilization of ancient Athens ended a couple of centuries after the Golden Age and the death of Alexander the Great. Of course, people still lived in the city and carried on nearly as before. But the city-states throughout Greece would never be independent again.

Even though the Greeks no longer had a strong political presence, Greek culture was not lost. In fact, the Romans—who conquered Greece in 146 BCE and made it a Roman province—borrowed much of their culture from Athens. Even today, the ideas, developments and inventions of ancient Athens still impact the lives of people in many Western countries.

Is it still possible to see remnants of ancient Greece today? Of course! If you were to visit Athens today here's some of what you would be able to see.

The Acropolis, the rocky hill and highest point in Athens, is still there. You must hike to the top of the Acropolis by walking along the ancient Panathenaia Way, the same route that the processional used to take during the Panathenaia Festival of ancient Athens.

On the top of the Acropolis stands the remains of the Parthenon. Parts have been demolished by people or have just worn away over time by erosion and air pollution. But most of it is still there. The Parthenon is one of the most popular places to visit in all of Athens and is one of the best examples of ancient Greek architecture left on Earth. The view from the

Acropolis is amazing, too. From here, you can look out over the beautiful city of Athens and see its ancient and modern architecture.[1]

The Parthenon isn't the only ancient structure on top of the Acropolis. On this "high city" stand a number of other ancient structures including the Erechtheum, a small temple honoring the mythical king Erechtheus. This building is famous for its Porch of the Maidens. The columns on this porch aren't designed in the traditional Doric, Ionic, or Corinthian style. Instead, they are in the shape of six female figures dressed in the traditional peplos of ancient Greece.[2]

On the southeastern slope of the Acropolis lies the ancient Theatre of Dionysus where the Athenians once performed their famous comedies and tragedies. There's not much left of the old theater today, though it once had around 20,000 seats. There are plans to restore this theater by the year 2015. Maybe someday you can even go there to watch a traditional Greek comedy or tragedy. But for today, you can just tour the ruins, sit on one of the original marble benches and imagine what the entertainment here would have been like.[3]

Very little remains of the agora or marketplace at the base of the Acropolis. Even so, these ruins are considered the best preserved of any agora in Greece. Visitors stroll the paths and read the placards which explain the use of each room and building. In the midst of the old agora stands a small replica of the marketplace, plus a museum showcasing some of the things that archaeologists have found on the site. On display are a variety of objects from the ancient world including pottery (such as amphoras), sculptures, clay lamps, coins, bronze objects, glass, and jewelry.[4]

Just outside the city of Athens, you can visit the site where Plato's Academy was located. During Plato's time, a direct road connected Athens to the Academy and students just walked back and forth when they needed to go to town. To get there today, you'll either take the metro (train) or ride in a car. When you arrive at the site, you'll see the remains of the old gymnasium, peristyle buildings (houses or apartments), and the sacred house.

The ancient harbor of Piraeus. It was connected to Athens by the Long Walls, which stretched for nearly seven miles.

You'll have to use your imagination since the old structures have long ago disappeared. When you walk through the gymnasium, picture ancient Greeks exercising and preparing for athletic competitions. As you step into the area that was once their apartments and houses, imagine students studying their texts written with the ancient Greek alphabet. Then, as you walk past the sacred house, think about what it might have been like for them to attend religious gatherings where they worshipped their gods. During your visit, keep in mind that you are tracing the footsteps of such great thinkers as Plato and Aristotle. It was along these paths and in these ancient rooms that many significant philosophical ideas were born.[5]

Once you've finished visiting these sites, you can end your visit to Athens by having a traditional dinner. After all, a trip to Athens just wouldn't be complete without a fine Greek meal. Athenians consider

A view of modern Athens. Lycabettus Hill, the city's highest point, is in the top center.

mealtime to be a very important part of their day. In Greek culture, it's not just about eating, though. It's about spending time with family and friends. Because of that, meals often last for hours.

Athenians, and Greeks in general, eat a lot of vegetables like cucumbers, tomatoes, cabbage, peas, eggplant, zucchini, onions, and potatoes. They also eat citrus fruits like lemons. Chickpeas (garbanzo beans) and olives are a big part of their diet, too. They love lamb, beef, fish, and chicken. And feta cheese, yogurt, honey, and pita bread are served at just about every meal.

If you are unable to travel to Athens, you can still taste some yummy traditional Greek food by making some at home. Several authentic Greek recipes have been included in the back of this book.

We hope you enjoy your meal. As they'd say in Athens, Kali Orexi (Bon Appétit)!

The Greek Alphabet

About 2000 BCE, the Minoans on the island of Crete developed a system of picture writing modeled after the hieroglyphs of ancient Egypt. It spread to mainland Greece. A thousand years later, the Greeks stopped keeping written records. No one knows why. Instead of communicating through writing, the people during this era relied on oral traditions told through stories and songs.

A Alpha (al-fah)	B Beta (bay-tah)	Γ Gamma (gam-ah)	Δ Delta (del-ta)	E Epsilon (ep-si-lon)	Z Zeta (zay-tah)
H Eta (ay-tah)	Θ Theta (thay-tah)	I Iota (eye-o-tah)	K Kappa (cap-pah)	Λ Lambda (lamb-dah)	M Mu (mew)
N Nu (new)	Ξ Xi (zie)	O Omicron (om-e-cron)	Π Pi (pie)	P Rho (roe)	Σ Sigma (sig-mah)
T Tau (taw)	Y Upsilon (up-si-lon)	Φ Phi (fie)	X Chi (kie)	Ψ Psi (sigh)	Ω Omega (oh-may-gah)

The Greek alphabet used by the students of Plato's Academy (still in use today) was developed around 800 BCE when the Greeks began trading with the Phoenicians—a people in modern-day Syria who developed the first alphabet. The Phoenician alphabet had 22 letters, all consonants. The Greek alphabet includes 24 letters, both consonants and vowels. In fact, the Greek alphabet was the first to include letters for vowel sounds. The vowels in the Greek alphabet are: A (alpha), E (epsilon and eta), I (iota), O (omicron and omega), and U (upsilon).

In addition to using the alphabet to write words, the Greeks also used letters to represent numbers. The first nine letters were 1 through 9, the next nine were multiples of 10, and the next nine letters were multiples of 100—for a total of 27 letters. Three letters were added to the end of the alphabet to accommodate the last three number values, though they aren't in use today.

You may recognize some Greek letters. These letters are used in the names of college fraternities and sororities. They are also used in science, engineering, and mathematics.

Greek Theater Masks

MATERIALS
- 2 dinner-size paper plates
- markers
- crayons
- hole-puncher
- scissors
- yarn
- glue
- stapler
- ribbons, plastic leaves and fake berries, pipe cleaners, and any other objects you'd like to use to decorate your mask.

DIRECTIONS
1. Punch two holes on the sides of the paper plates. Tie a piece of yarn to each hole. These will be used to tie around your head to hold the mask in place.
2. Carefully cut circles for the mouth and eyes of your mask.
3. Decorate the mask using ideas found in these illustrations or those found online. Remember, Greek masks had really animated expressions. If the character was sad, they REALLY made the mask look sad. If the character was surprised or happy, they REALLY made the mask look surprised or happy. The audience had to be able to tell what the character was feeling just by looking at the mask.
4. To decorate the mask, use any of the suggested supplies, or come up with your own ideas. Attach them to the mask with glue or a stapler, whichever works better for you.

Authentic Greek Recipes: Sweetmeats

These would have been served as little desserts or as snacks in between courses at a special dinner.

INGREDIENTS

½ cup sesame seeds
4 tablespoons honey

DIRECTIONS

1. Pour the sesame seeds and honey into a saucepan and stir.
2. Simmer on low heat until the mixture is slightly thickened and a rich, golden color.
3. To see if the mixture is ready, drop a spoonful onto a damp plate. Let it cool slightly. Then work the mixture into a ball. If it keeps its shape, the mixture is ready. If it doesn't, it needs to cook a bit longer.
4. When the mixture is ready, take the pan off the stove. Keep stirring the mixture until it is cool.
5. Wet your hands with water. Scoop a tablespoon of the mixture into your hands and roll it into a ball. Wrap in waxed paper. Continue until you've used all of the mixture. You should be able to make 20–25 sweetmeats.

Authentic Greek Recipes: Hummus

Remember how the ancient Athenians used to scoop up their food with pieces of bread? That's exactly what you get to do with this yummy dip. Serve it with pita bread cut into triangles.

INGREDIENTS
1   (15-ounce) can garbanzo beans, drained, liquid reserved
1   clove garlic, crushed
2   teaspoons ground cumin
½   teaspoon salt
2   tablespoons lemon juice
¼   cup olive oil
½   onion, chopped fine
⅔   cup feta cheese, chopped fine
1   tablespoon dried oregano
2   tablespoons olive oil

DIRECTIONS
1. Combine all ingredients into a blender or food processor.
2. Blend on low until smooth and creamy.

Greek Salad with Feta Cheese

The ancient Greeks wouldn't have had tomatoes (they weren't discovered until Columbus found them in the Americas). Yet, the rest of the ingredients in this dish would have been typical for an ancient Greek side dish. Serve it with bread you can dip in olive oil.

INGREDIENTS

3   medium tomatoes, cut into cubes
1   cucumber, cut into cubes
2   green peppers, chopped into small pieces
    Olive oil
    Oregano
    Black olives (optional)

DIRECTIONS

Place first 6 ingredients into a salad bowl and mix well. Then, stir in oregano and olive oil. Add more olive oil and oregano if desired.

BCE

6000–3000   Neolithic Era. Greek civilization is believed to begin.

3000–1000   The Bronze Age. Greeks first begin using bronze to make tools, art pieces, craft items, and weapons. Two primary groups of people live in Greece. Minoans live on the island of Crete, while Mycenaeans live on the mainland of Greece.

2000–1000   The Minoans develop two forms of writing: Linear A and Linear B.

1700–1400   The famous palace of Knossos is built on the island of Crete.

1250   The Trojan War begins. Greek soldiers hidden in a wooden horse help defeat the city of Troy after a 10-year siege.

1100   Dorians attack mainland Mycenaean Greece. Art, writing, and other advanced skills are temporarily lost.

1000–800   The Greek Dark Ages. No written records exist from this time period since few people know how to read and write. Legends are passed on through songs and stories.

800–700   Greeks begin decorating pottery with geometric shapes which show influences from the Far East.

776   The first Olympic Games are held at Olympia.

750   Homer writes his two famous poems *The Iliad* and *The Odyssey.*

600   Solon creates a constitution in Athens and helps the city get out of debt by cultivating a new crop, olives.

550   Persian Empire begins under leadership of Cyrus the Great.

508   Cleisthenes gains support of Athenians and Athenian democracy begins.

490   Athenians defeat invading Persians at the Battle of Marathon. According to legend, a runner travels from Marathon to Athens (22 miles) to give news of the victory and dies after delivering the news. The modern-day marathon is derived from this legend.

483	Athenian leader Themistocles persuades his fellow citizens to build a fleet of warships.
480	Persians attack Greece, but are defeated at the naval Battle of Salamis, involving the warships the Athenians have recently constructed and contributions from other city states.
479–323	Classical Period or The Golden Age. Greek civilization reaches its peak, as arts, sports, architecture, philosophy, and more all flourish.
469	Socrates is born in Athens.
460	Pericles becomes a dominant Athenian politician.
447	Construction on the Parthenon begins.
431	The Peloponnesian War between Athens and Sparta begins.
429	Plato is born in Athens. He is eventually taught by Socrates and becomes a teacher of Aristotle.
415	Athens invades Sicily and suffers a disastrous defeat.
404	Sparta conquers Athens after 27 years of fighting as the Peloponnesian War ends.
399	Socrates is forced to drink poison and dies.
387	Plato founds his philosophical school called the Academy.
384	Aristotle is born in Athens. He is eventually taught by Plato and becomes a teacher of Alexander the Great.
356	Alexander the Great is born.
347	Plato dies.
331–323	Alexander the Great spreads Greek culture from Egypt to India.
146	Greece becomes a Roman province; many Greek traditions become part of the Roman way of life.

Chapter 1: A Grand Celebration

1. Bear Rowell, "Global Timeline: The Great Panathenaea." *Mekeel's & Stamps Magazine,* August 13, 2004, p. 19.
2. Roger Dunkle, "The Panathenaic Festival." http://depthome.brooklyn.cuny.edu/classics/dunkle/courses/panfest/panfest.htm
3. John Fleischman, "In classical Athens, a market trading in the currency of ideas." *Smithsonian,* July 1993, p. 38.
4. Roger Dunkle, "The Panathenaic Festival." http://depthome.brooklyn.cuny.edu/classics/dunkle/courses/panfest/panfest.htm

Chapter 2: A City Protected by Athena

1. Paul Cartledge, "The Democratic Experiment," BBC History. http://www.bbc.co.uk/history/ancient/greeks/greekdemocracy_01.shtml
2. Ibid.
3. CIA, *The World Factbook*: Greece https://www.cia.gov/library/publications/the-world-factbook/fields/2060.html?countryName=Greece&countryCode=gr&regionCode=eu&#gr
4. Michael Gagarin and Elaine Fantham, *Oxford Encyclopedia of Ancient Greece and Rome, Volume 1.* New York: Oxford University Press, 2010.
5. Sara Ann McGill, *Ancient Greece Timeline.* Toledo, Ohio: Great Neck Publishing, 2009.
6. Charles Anthon and William Smith. *A New Classical Dictionary of Greek and Roman Biography, Mythology, and Geography.* Harper and Brothers, 1860, pp. 118-119.

Chapter 3: Life in Athens

1. Leonidas C. Polopolus. "Athens, Greece: A City-State that grew from Optimality in the Golden Era." http://www.clas.ufl.edu/users/kapparis/AOC/ATHENS.htm
2. Women in Classical Greece, Metropolitan Museum of Art. http://www.metmuseum.org/toah/hd/wmna/hd_wmna.htm
3. "Daily Life in Ancient Greece," The British Museum. http://www.ancientgreece.co.uk/dailylife/challenge/cha_set.html
4. Dimitris Kyrtatas, "The Athenian democracy and its slaves." *History Today,* February 1994, Vol. 44, Issue 2.
5. Maggie Riechers, "Growing Up in Ancient Greece." *Humanities,* July/August 2003, Vol. 24, Issue 4, pp. 30–33.

6. Jennifer Neils, "Picturing Ancient Greek Childhood." *Antiques,* October 2003, p.127.

7. Ibid.

8. Jeri DeBrohun, "Power Dressing in Ancient Greece and Rome." *History Today,* February 2001, Vol. 51, Issue 2, p. 18.

9. "Daily Life in Ancient Greece," The British Museum. http://www.ancientgreece.co.uk/dailylife/challenge/cha_set.html

10. John Fleischman, "In classical Athens, a market trading in the currency of ideas." *Smithsonian,* July 1993, p. 38.

Chapter 4: The Golden Age

1. The Athenian Agora
   http://www.agathe.gr/overview/

2. John Fleischman, "In classical Athens, a market trading in the currency of ideas." *Smithsonian,* July 1993, p. 38.

3. Josephine Delvey,"Hippocrates." San Jose State University.
   http://www.sjsu.edu/depts/Museum/hippoc.html

4. John L. Tomkinson, "Classical Athens I. The Golden Age." *Anagnosis* Books. http://www.anagnosis.gr/index.php?pageID=202&la=eng

5. "What's this." *Dig,* October 2011, Vol. 13, Issue 8, pp. 34–35.

6. Greek Sculpture, BBC: How Art Made the World
   http://www.youtube.com/watch?v=88gXWW3qN7o

Chapter 5: Visiting Ancient Athens

1. Athens Info Guide
   http://www.athensinfoguide.com/wtsacrop.htm

2. Rick Steves' Europe_Athens and Side Trips
   http:www.dailymotion.com/video/
   xatnrf_rick-steves-europe-athens-and-side_travel

3. "Ancient Theatre under Acropolis to be restored." *BBC News,* November 26, 2009. http://news.bbc.co.uk/2/hi/entertainment/8380307.stm

4. Museum of Ancient Agora
   http://odysseus.culture.gr/h/1/eh151.jsp?obj_id=3290

5. Athens Info Guide
   http://www.athensinfoguide.com/wtsacrop.htm

"Athens, city, Greece." *Columbia Electronic Encyclopedia, 6th Edition,* July 1, 2010, pp. 1–3.

"Athens divine city." *WE Magazine,* March/April 1999, Vol. 3, Issue 2, p. 36.

Baker, Charles F. "Judging Right and Wrong in Athens." *Calliope,* October, 2008.

Cartledge, Paul. "The Democratic Experiment." BBC History, http://www.bbc.co.uk/history/ancient/greeks/greekdemocracy_01.shtml

CIA, *The World Factbook,* Greece https://www.cia.gov/library/publications/the-world-factbook/fields/2060.html?countryName=Greece&countryCode=gr&regionCode=eu&#gr

Davis, William Stearns. *A Day in Old Athens.* Norwood, MA: Norwood Press, 1914.

DeBrohun, Jeri. "Power Dressing in Ancient Greece and Rome." *History Today.* February 2001, Vol. 51 Issue 2, p. 18.

Delvey, Josephine. "Hippocrates." San Jose State University. http://www.sjsu.edu/depts/Museum/hippoc.html

Dunkle, Roger. "Panathenaic Festival." http://depthome.brooklyn.cuny.edu/classics/dunkle/courses/panfest/panfest.htm

Eastman, Jennifer. "Athens." Our World: Greece, 2010, p. 2.

Fleischman, John. "In classical Athens, a market trading in the currency of ideas." *Smithsonian,* July 1993, Vol. 24, Issue 4, p. 38.

Neils, Jennifer and Stephen V. Tracy. "The Games at Athens." *Excavations of the Athenian Agora.* Athens: The American School of Classical Studies at Athens, 2003. http://www.agathe.gr/Icons/pdfs/AgoraPicBk-25.pdf

On the Internet

"Ancient Theatre under Acropolis to be restored. "*BBC News,* November 26, 2009. http://news.bbc.co.uk/2/hi/entertainment/8380307.stm

Anthon, Charles and William Smith. *A New Classical Dictionary of Greek and Roman Biography, Mythology, and Geography."* New York: Harper and Brothers, 1860.

Athenian Agora http://www.agathe.gr/overview/

Glossary

agora (uh-gor-UH)—Marketplace.

amphora (AM-for-uh)—Large two-handled ceramic storage jar with an oval body and a pair of handles.

architecture (AHR-ki-tek-cher)—The character or style of buildings.

cerulean (suh-ROO-lee-uhn)—Deep blue.

chariots (CHAIR-ee-uts)—Two-wheeled horse-drawn vehicles.

chitons (KYE-tuhnz)—Knee-length linen or wool robes worn by Greek men.

Corinthian (kuh-RIN-thee-uhn)—One of three types of columns used in Greek and later Roman architecture that has a capital (top) decorated with leaves, scrolls, and flowers.

democracy (dih-MOK-ruh-see)—Government by the people.

Doric (DOOR-ick)—The earliest type of column used in Greek architecture that is the most plain of all the Greek columns and thicker and heavier.

edifice (EH-duh-fuss)—A large, imposing building.

feta (FEHT-uh)—Soft, white very flavorful cheese made out of goat's milk.

Ionic (eye-AWN-ick)—One of three types of columns used in Greek architecture (Doric is earlier and Corinthian is later). It is characterized by having a scroll-shaped ornament at the top of the column.

javelin (JAV-uh-lin)—Light spear usually thrown by hand.

mythology (mih-THOL-uh-jee)—A set of stories, traditions, and beliefs of a particular group of people.

peplos (PEP-luhs)—Ankle-length linen or wool robe worn by Greek women.

peristyle (PARE-uh-style)—Row of columns around a building that enclose a courtyard.

philosophy (fih-LOS-uh-fee)—The investigation of truths and principles of being, knowledge, and conduct.

pita (PEE-tuh)—A round, flat bread common in the Mediterranean and Middle Eastern cultures.

pomegranates (POM-uh-gran-its)—Fruit filled with juicy, red, edible seeds.

sculpture (SKUHLP-cher)—The art of carving, molding, welding, or otherwise producing three-dimensional works of art.

symposium (sim-POH-zee-uhm)—In ancient Greece and Rome, a meeting following dinner that included intellectual conversation.